MW00629041

Published by Lone Valley Publishing,
Campbellsville, KY 42718

© 2013 by Ray Hollenbach All rights reserved.
Published in e-format 2012

ISBN-10: 0-9882787-5-8

ISBN-13: 978-0-9882787-5-2

Unless otherwise noted, all Scripture quotations are from
New International Version, Copyright 1973, 1978, 1984
by International Bible Society and published by
Zondervan.

Twenty-Five Days of Christmas (In One Minute or Less)

A Christmas devotional for incredibly busy people

By Ray Hollenbach

Dedication

This is for you, the reader:

I get it: you're in a hurry.

Christmas means more things to do: all the daily stuff of living, plus the pressures of a holiday.

Go ahead, skip the introduction. It's way too long.

Jump right to the devotions, you can read each one in less than a minute.

But be careful, Christmas may never be the same.

Introduction: *The God of Nobodies*

When really important people come to town, everyone one knows it. NBA stadiums sell out months before LeBron or Kobe show up for game time. When Kristen Stewart and Robert Pattinson do a personal appearance, hundreds of screaming fans will show up hours ahead of time. When the President visits your city, you can be sure the mayor will meet him at the airport and school children will be there to give the first lady flowers.

But the Christmas story shows us God does things differently. You might even call his way sneaky. The most important person in the history of the world snuck into town late one night and definitely did not stay in a five-star hotel. Jesus was smuggled into Bethlehem through the womb of a teenage girl, who gave birth in a barn. That's different.

We all know the story of Christmas: the baby, the barn, the shepherds and magi. Hidden inside that familiar story is the surprising revelation that God's way is to ignore the bigshots and use nobodies instead. Just count the nobodies:

Mary was a teenage girl from a small town. In Bible times women were not important people, and teenagers were even lower on the scale. Mix in her pre-martial pregnancy, and you've got a real nobody on your hands. But Mary was God's choice. She conceived the baby Jesus through the power of the Holy Spirit. God considered her somebody important and gave her a pretty tough assignment!

Joseph was a nobody, too. He was just a working man across town from Mary's family. He was faced with a choice between trusting God or protecting his small-town reputation. But reputations belong to important people, and most of the important people were in Jerusalem. Joseph said "yes" to shame, yes to love, and yes to God, so God chose Joseph to act as a foster-father to the Savior of the world.

Shepherds are not important people. Just the opposite: second-shift schmucks who work outdoors. Back in that day watching sheep was not exactly a rock-star kind of gig. Yet they were the first guests invited to the celebration.

The Magi? Nothing more than rich pagan astrologers. It didn't matter if they had money, they were foreigners. Foreigners have the wrong religion, the wrong clothes, and the wrong sacred books. **Elizabeth & Zechariah**: a kindly old couple engaged in harmless religious activity. They are the kind of people society ignores—unless they are driving too slowly on the highway. **Anna & Simeon**: Alone and elderly, they were two people almost completely invisible to everyone. Everyone except the Holy Spirit.

One and all, God used people on the outside of society.

The secret message inside the Christmas story? God invites the nobodies. And when God invites you to the table, he provides everything you need. The powerful people, the beautiful people, and the cool kids might not make it to the celebration. They're welcome, but they might be too busy building their own kingdoms. Meanwhile God's kingdom is filling up with the people no one notices.

This season, if you are a nobody—rejoice! You are not far from the Kingdom of God.

*Twenty-Five Days of Christmas
(In One Minute or Less)*

From the Life of Mary:

DAY ONE
In the sixth month, God sent the angel Gabriel
to Nazareth, a town in Galilee, to a virgin
pledged to be married to a man named Joseph,
a descendant of David. The virgin's name was
Mary. (Luke 1:26-27)

In the sixth month . . . God's clock was already
ticking when the angel came to Mary. Just
because God announces something *to me*
doesn't mean it began *with me*.

From the Life of Mary:

DAY TWO
*In the sixth month, God sent the angel Gabriel
to Nazareth, a town in Galilee, to a virgin
pledged to be married to a man named Joseph,
a descendant of David. The virgin's name was
Mary. (Luke 1:26-27)*

pledged to be married . . . We have our plans.
God has his. What happens when his plans
overtake ours? God's plans for our lives always
involve adapting—or even setting aside—our
plans. How flexible are you?

From the Life of Mary:

DAY THREE
*The angel went to her and said, "Greetings, you who are highly favored! The Lord is with you."
(Luke 1:28)*

You who are highly favored! The Lord is with you . . . Notice the connection between his favor and his presence. How could it be otherwise? This is the only definition of God's favor we really need, and it's the promise he makes most often, "I will be with you."

From the Life of Mary:

DAY FOUR
Mary was greatly troubled at his words and wondered what kind of greeting this might be. (Luke 1:29)

Mary was greatly troubled at his words . . . It can be unsettling when his favor is upon us. We may not even know what it's all about. Yet even in our ignorance we can find comfort: his presence and favor will change our little world forever. Although change can be difficult, God's changes are always for the better.

From the Life of Mary:

DAY FIVE
*"Do not be afraid, Mary, you have found favor
with God. You will be with child and give birth
to a son, and you are to give him the name
Jesus." (Luke 1:30-31)*

You will be with child . . . Sometimes we
volunteer for the purposes of God, and
sometimes we are drafted. Either way, his
purpose for us is filled with favor. Why do you
think the angel mentions God's favor a second
time?

From the Life of Mary:

DAY SIX
"How will this be," Mary asked the angel, *"since I am a virgin?"* (Luke 1:34)

How will this be? . . . There is a world of difference between asking God *how* and asking him *why*. To ask *how* is to focus on going forward. Sometimes asking *why* is a way to wrestle for control.

From the Life of Mary:

DAY SEVEN
The angel answered, "The Holy Spirit will come upon you, and the power of the Most High will overshadow you. So the holy one to be born will be called the Son of God. (Luke 1:35)

The Holy Spirit will come upon you . . . When God answers the "how" question, this is the usual way he starts: what he commands, he empowers—and he empowers through the intimate presence of his Holy Spirit, alive in us.

From the Life of Mary:

DAY EIGHT
For nothing is impossible with God (Luke 1:37)

For nothing is impossible with God . . . That's right: you heard him. Or was it only true back then?

From the Life of Mary:

DAY NINE
"I am the Lord's servant," Mary answered. "May it be to me as you have said." Then the angel left her. (Luke 1:38)

I am the Lord's servant . . . *Even* though Mary was drafted, she responds with a willing heart. It could not have been an easy task to embrace, especially in that very moment. What empowered her response was the fact that her identity was already secure: she saw herself as "the Lord's servant."

From the Life of Mary:

DAY TEN
Then the angel left her. (Luke 1:38)

Then the angel left her . . . There are times when we have angelic help, and there are times when we are on our own. Wouldn't it have been better if the angel stuck around to help explain things to Mary's loved ones? Why do you think the angel left?

From the Life of Joseph:

DAY ELEVEN
"Mary was pledged to be married to Joseph, but before they came together, she was found to be with child through the Holy Spirit." (Matthew 1:18)

Poor Joseph—God didn't get his approval before acting. Joseph received the worst news of his life: his hopes and dreams for a wife and family came to a dreadful halt. Before Joseph could follow God's path, he had to decide if he was on the side of propriety, or scandal. What do you think: are these the only two choices he faced?

From the Life of Joseph:

DAY TWELVE
Because Joseph her husband was a righteous man and did not want to expose her to public disgrace, he had in mind to divorce her quietly. (Matthew 1:19)

The narrative shows us what a righteous man looks like. In his confusion and pain, Joseph's first concern was for Mary. How many of us would have this priority? Perhaps this is why the scripture labels him a "righteous man." Joseph's righteousness is rendered not in terms of his relationship to God, but in terms of his relationship to Mary. True righteousness extends two directions—toward God *and* toward others.

From the Life of Joseph:

DAY THIRTEEN
After he had considered this, an angel of the Lord appeared to him (Matthew 1:20)

Joseph resisted the urge to act rashly. Even though Joseph did not want to disgrace Mary he was still determined to break the engagement. Yet the narrative reveals that he took time to *consider* his actions. He was faced with impossible disappointment and heartbreak, but he did not rush to judgment. We don't know how long he waited, but he took time to consider his actions. In that period of time, Joseph *positioned himself* to hear from God. Do our snap judgments keep us from hearing God?

From the Life of Joseph:

DAY FOURTEEN
An angel of the Lord appeared to him in a dream and said, 'Joseph son of David, do not be afraid to take Mary home as your wife.' (Matthew 1:20)

God gave Joseph a dream, one that would change his life forever. This must've been some dream! Engagement, an unexpected pregnancy, and an out-of-this-world explanation would be enough to give anyone dreams. Sill, God chose a dream as the means to provide divine direction, and Joseph recognized the dream as God's personal leading. Consider this: there is no indication that Joseph heard anything else from God until after the baby was born. He remained faithful to God's instructions for months, all based on one dream!

From the Lives of the Shepherds

DAY FIFTEEN
*There were shepherds living out in the fields
nearby, keeping watch over their flocks at night.
An angel of the Lord appeared to them, and the
glory of the Lord shone around them . . .
Suddenly a great company of the heavenly host
appeared with the angel, singing"* (Luke 2:8-9,
and 13)

First, a single angel announced glad tidings of
great joy to the shepherds on the hillside. Then
the host of heaven appeared, singing, "Glory to
God in the highest, and on earth peace to men
on whom his favor rests." Heaven is comprised
of a community of worship. Whatever God
does, it is accompanied by communal worship.
The shepherds were invited to join in, and so
are we. Praise and adoration go hand in hand
with the work of God. We, too, are invited to be
a part of this community of worship.

From the Lives of the Shepherds

DAY SIXTEEN
*Suddenly a great company of the heavenly host
appeared with the angel. (Matthew 2:9)*

The resources of heaven: that night on a
Bethlehem hillside, a multitude of the heavenly
host was employed to lead a handful of
shepherds to the feet of Jesus. One angel
would've been enough! In this act God
demonstrates that the resources of heaven are
always available to lead people to Christ. Have
we called upon the resources of heaven, or do
we merely rely on our own?

*The Christmas stories are filled with revelation of how God works in our world, whether it's Christmas Day or any day. For example, have you ever considered **How God Speaks?***

DAY SEVENTEEN

God speaks through angels: Angels spoke to Mary, Joseph, and the shepherds. Our very word *angel* comes from the Greek, *ángelos,* meaning *messenger*. While the birth of Jesus was certainly unique in history, God's use of angels is anything but unique--they exist carry his messages and do his work. Church history is filled with accounts of angelic visitation. What if God wanted to use an angel to speak to you? Are you open to the possibility of an angelic visitation today?

How God Speaks

DAY EIGHTEEN

God speaks through dreams: The record shows that God spoke to Joseph exclusively through dreams. What's more, Joseph took these dreams seriously and made life-altering choices based on them. Would *you* marry someone or move to a foreign country based on your dreams? Joseph did! In fact, we are in the habit of referring to "*our dreams*," but what if they are God's? Dreams are mentioned no fewer than four times in Matthew's Christmas narrative. The scripture demonstrates God can and does guide his children through dreams. Imagine: in an emotionally charged situation like the Nativity, just when we would be tempted to ignore our dreams as a product of our subconscious, God is present: leading, directing, and guiding—through dreams.

How God Speaks

DAY NINETEEN

God speaks through nature: Matthew's Christmas narrative also tells the story of the Magi: three pagan wise men who spent time and energy in search of the newborn king. The wise men bowed in worship before the infant Jesus. They were literally moved to action because of what they observed in nature. Who would pack up their treasures and travel over deserts and mountains based on what they had seen in the sky? The Magi heard the voice—or saw the hand—of God and set out to find the King of Israel, all because God spoke through nature. What has creation whispered to you?

How God Speaks

DAY TWENTY
All this took place to fulfill what the Lord said through the prophet . . . (Matthew 1:22)

God speaks through the scripture: Matthew takes great care to point out the fulfillment of Old Testament prophecy in his nativity story. The stars may have guided the wise men to Israel, but the words of the prophet Micah gave them the final steps to take (Matthew 2:1-6). Even Mary's spontaneous song of praise in Luke's gospel, known as *The Magnificat,* is based on the words recorded in the Old Testament nearly a thousand years before. The Christmas story is filled with references to the Bible passages of old. In our day many people study the Bible, but how many hear his voice in it?

How God Speaks

DAY TWENTY-ONE

God speaks through governments: The opening words of Luke's Christmas gospel mention Caesar Augustus' decree that all the world be taxed (Luke 2:1). Grumbling taxpayers everywhere did not hear anything other than the greed of Rome, but behind the machinations of politics and taxation God was moving people from one city to the next in order to set his plan in motion. So the next time you read about a new tax, be sure to check for God's voice!

How God Speaks

DAY TWENTY-TWO
*Now there was a man in Jerusalem named
Simeon, who was righteous and devout. He was
waiting for the consolation of Israel, and the
Holy Spirit was upon him. (Luke 2:25)*

God speaks through the Holy Spirit: Two
elderly people named Simeon and Anna are
almost forgotten from the Christmas story these
days. They received the most unusual kind of
invitation to celebrate the birth of King Jesus—
they had a hunch! What we might call a hunch
was really the voice of the Holy Spirit. Luke's
account makes it clear that these two obscure
temple-dwellers heard the still small voice of the
Spirit, right down the to time and place where
Joseph and Mary would come to the Temple to
dedicate the baby Jesus. Could our lives be
guided like that? The scripture suggests they can.

How God Speaks

DAY TWENTY-THREE

God speaks through prophetic utterance:
There's another character hidden away in the Christmas story. His name is Zechariah, the father of John the Baptist (Did you know John the Baptist was also a part of the Christmas story? It would take longer than a minute to fill you in!). It's a long story, but Zechariah spent nine months without the use of his voice. When he finally opened his mouth after nine months of silence, he prophesied! When Mary met Zechariah's wife, Elizabeth, the courtyard of their simple house became the gathering of saints, and both women spoke the words of God. The Christmas narrative is telling us that when God is at work, God's people will speak inspired words of life. That should change the way we listen to one another, don't you think?

How God Speaks

DAY TWENTY-FOUR
The Word became flesh and made his dwelling among us. (John 1:14)

Finally, **God speaks through Jesus**: The Christ Child is the "Word become flesh." The grand opening of John's gospel reveals the Word was with God, and the Word was God. The opening of the book of Hebrews reveals that although God speaks in many times and in many ways, his ultimate word to us is a person: Jesus (Hebrews 1:1-2). The angels told the shepherds, *"This shall be a sign for you: you will find a baby . . ."* All of God's words are contained in Jesus. They were then. They are still.

DAY TWENTY-FIVE, CHRISTMAS DAY:

The Parable That is Christmas

God comes to us in unexpected ways. Our
problem is that we are looking for him
according to our expectations. This is one of the
lessons of the first Christmas: God came to
nation that eagerly longed for his coming,
prayed for his return, and placed all their hopes
in his presence. Yet most of the nation missed
the hour of his visitation. Is this simply history,
or a parable for our day?

Israel had looked for a "day of visitation" for at
least 500 years before the coming of Jesus. The
nation remembered the golden age of King
David a thousand years before the days of
Herod, a counterfeit king. David was the
prototype of God's chosen vessel, a unifying and
conquering King who established Israel in
peace, security, and prosperity. After David's
reign many the prophets began to anticipate a
day when *Yahweh*, the God of Israel, would not
rule through a representative king. Instead, God
would come personally, take his place on earth,

and establish Jerusalem as the pinnacle of the earth.

The day of God's visitation would be both glorious and terrifying. The oppressed (Israel) would be rescued and the oppressor (Persia, Syria, Greece, Rome--or whoever was on top at the time) would be cast down. The people of Israel were looking for their freedom and expected God to judge the rest of the world as well. They expected God would come to the Temple and establish his throne on the earth. They expected "The Day of the Lord," great and terrible--great for them, terrible for their enemies. These expectations were based on their understanding of the scriptures and the encouragement of their teachers. These expectations shaped their view of the world, and became the substance of their hopes.

Who could have imagined that when God came to earth personally, he would be dressed in frailty? Who could have imagined that God would indeed come to the Temple, only to declare that the true Temple was built of living stones? Who could have imagined that this King would establish his throne in the hearts of men?

And perhaps most incredibly, who could have imagined that the Day of Judgment would indeed come, but that the Son of God would take the judgment upon himself in order to save the guilty?

Of course, in our day, we know these things. We can see clearly. But still the original question remains as a Christmas meditation: Is this simply history, or a parable for our day?

AND WHAT ABOUT ALL THE OTHER DAYS,
THE ONES FOLLOWING CHRISTMAS DAY?

Epilogue: The Lesson of Christmas

Some things hide in plain sight. Others hide
behind fancy names. And still others hide
among the over-decorated trappings of tradition
dressed up as garish holiday cheer. Sometimes
it's all three.

The truth about Christmas is that God became a
man. The transcendent Creator of the Universe,
the One who sits outside his creation submerged
himself in the work of his hands. The Playwright
walked on stage during the show. The Coach
became a player. The King became a
commoner.
He wasn't a Poser, pretending to be something
other than what he was: he was born, and he
grew; he came of age and took his place among
us; he embraced his purpose and fulfilled it
completely. He wasn't slumming among us like
some impostor: he laughed, he cried, he sweat.
When we struck him, he bled. When we pierced
him, he died.

Something as grand and wonderful as Christmas certainly has many sub-themes: peace on earth, goodwill toward men, hope for tomorrow, salvation for all, and the fulfillment of promise. We should listen to each line of the symphony and enjoy the beauty of each one. Put them all together than they point to the grand melody, that God became man.

When God became man, he demonstrated how to be human. His life, in the person of Jesus Christ, is the model of all lives, everywhere and in every time. Men from every age can look to Jesus has example. Women from every culture can discover fullness in him. God did not cheat the game by walking through life untouched by the trouble we face. He faced the same troubles we have faced, and indeed more, because to his trouble was added unique rejection of all mankind toward him. Humanity had never seen his type before, and the one encounter between God and humanity resulted in our utter rejection of him, but he responded with un-rejectable love.

You can have your shepherds, wise men, angels, and mangers. For me, the grandeur of Christmas is captured in the gospel, which places its cards on the table right from the start:

The true light that gives light to everyone was coming into the world. He was in the world, and though the world was made through him, the world did not recognize him. He came to that which was his own, but his own did not receive him. Yet to all who did receive him, to those who believed in his name, he gave the right to become children of God— children born not of natural descent, nor of human decision or a husband's will, but born of God. The Word became flesh and made his dwelling among us. We have seen his glory, the glory of the one and only Son, who came from the Father, full of grace and truth. (John 1:9-14)

John tells us plainly, "*No one has ever seen God, but the one and only Son, who is himself God and is in closest relationship with the Father, has made him known.*" (John 1: 18)

What does God look like? He looks like Jesus. The Father *spoke himself* in Jesus. The countless words of every generation, arrayed in questions, arguments, songs and poems have been answered in the single Word, Jesus. The same

Word that spoke creation into being speaks life into us today.

When God became man, it looked like Jesus, and it still does. If we aspire to the presence of God in our everyday, we are really aspiring to Jesus. Because he is human we have the hope of his likeness. Because he is God, we have the certainty of his promise. All other messages flow from the Word made flesh. He was announced as Emmanuel, and he continues to reveal himself as such: God is forever with us because he has forever pitched his tent in the person of Jesus, the true lesson of Christmas.

Made in the USA
Lexington, KY
10 November 2019

56709591R00026